LEAVING THE ABBEY

LEAVING THE

ABBEY:

Reflections on a Several-Year, Parallel Journey
of a Christian Parish and a Group of Wonderful Women
(plus Monks)

KATHRYN H–F

WestBow
PRESS
A DIVISION OF THOMAS NELSON

WestBow Press books may be ordered through booksellers or by contacting:

WestBow Press
A Division of Thomas Nelson
1663 Liberty Drive
Bloomington, IN 47403
www.westbowpress.com
1-(866) 928-1240

ISBN: 978-1-4497-8794-3 (sc)
ISBN: 978-1-4497-8795-0 (hc)
ISBN: 978-1-4497-8796-7 (e)

Library of Congress Control Number: 2013904367

Printed in the United States of America

WestBow Press rev. date: 3/25/2013

DEDICATION

For Dad, T.J., and Irene…together again.

TABLE OF CONTENTS

FOREWORD

ife is a revealing process, a series of events whose outlook can only be clarified once one becomes involved in the process. So often our lot is such that one never knows where sequences of events connect and intertwine themselves into the realm of reason unless they become engaged in one's own existence. Try and try as we do, we are exposed to new things that have been carefully, insightfully choreographed by the great Designer of life. There are no accidents – there is only orchestration. We are part of God's **work of perfection.**

Perfection - not as defined in western culture as the opposite of imperfection, void of defects and such -but as the total sum of our ability to look upon our life experiences and learn from them.

In Ephesians 2:10, the apostle Paul wrote these powerful words: "For we are his workmanship, created in Christ Jesus for good works, which God prepared beforehand, that we should walk in them." (RSV) The word **workmanship** signifies "art work." We are God's work of art – he incorporates our lives into each and every stroke of his Divine brush.

Such is the tale of personal reflections contained within Kathryn's story. It is aptly subtitled: a **Parallel Journey.** How often can it be said that we are attentive of all peripheral activities leading toward a centralizing point of piecing together? In her own personal introspective recollection, Kathryn weaves three strands together making one braid: the journey of a parish, a group of wonderful women, plus monks. What do they all have in common with one another? They are all on a journey, whose trajectory no one was able to see and yet all had to succumb to something other, bigger and greater than themselves. This journey is one of refinement and conviction as they all strive for the same end.

The telling from Kathryn's vocational passage resonates with our own quest for meaning and purpose – how God carefully weaves things in and out of our lives, not through randomless, trivial acts but insightfully and creatively. His highest aim is to fashion godly character in all of us as a way of perfecting His image in us. The Scriptures tell us that we are made in God's image. We, however, cloud that reflection when life's arduous realities chip away at such a model of beauty. At times we become frustrated with others, ourselves, and even God – but as is so fittingly put in *Leaving the Abbey*, there is a peace that comes from a struggle well-struggled. Anything that requires effort is worthwhile, especially when that worthwhileness demands the sacrifice of uncertainty in order to conquer the fear of the unknown.

The truth is we are not walking into the unknown, but the known. Christ comes to meet us where we are and takes us to where He is, where we need to be. He brings us to a place He already has prepared, specifically for us. Christ does not make us go where He is unsure of – he takes us to where He is: complete.

Completeness comes in the most unassuming of ways, subtly when a new day of hope dawns after the darkest night of the soul. Only when we empty ourselves of all human pretension, allowing God to get us out of our ways, can we distinguish what is truly right, noble and worthy of effort. Though the cost is truly costly, what is good will bring about fruit commendable of our labor.

Kathryn's journey is our journey – it is a story of braiding – reflections from the heart, how God braids the strands of life's experiences together into the most elusive of human qualities: trust.

I pray, trust and hope that *Leaving the Abbey* will be of some help to you in bringing further spiritual power to current, everyday life.

Rev. Gus Calvo
Pastor of St. George's Anglican Church, Helmetta NJ

PREFACE

I n constructing this book I drew from the stories of two separate groups, each faced with the prospect of unwelcome departure from a beloved home. I am a part of both groups, one a former Episcopal (now Anglican) parish in New Jersey, the other as member of the Matt Talbot Retreat Movement, specifically Group W-32, Medallion #207. This latter collection of a fairly diverse group of women (that would explain the W) is unified by our being "in recovery from alcohol." We are all trying to move closer to Godly perfection, in our own sometimes intertwining ways.

OK, about the monks. When I joined Retreat Group W-32 in January 8ᵗʰ of 1989, I received my Medallion #207 at the Queen of Peace Retreat House at St. Paul's Abbey, a Benedictine community. I knew a little bit about monastic life from college courses in religious history, but knew little about Benedict himself. Curiosity has started many a quest. I moved from a condensed paperback version to the reference I'm using here, *St. Benedict's Rule,* the 2004 second edition. The impatient modern reader will be happy to find it composed of short chapters devoted to a single Rule (referenced as RB, for Rule of Benedict, with its number and paragraph if applicable, e.g., RB 6.2). These provided inspiration for the fond or profound memories related herein. Chapter 4 of the *Rule* lists "Guidelines for Christian and Monastic Good Practice." You see, Benedict felt the laity would benefit from the *Rule*; he viewed it as but a beginning toward perfection. It describes in essence a life of obedience to an authority that you trust absolutely. But coming to that trust could take most of a lifetime.

Yet even now a significant number of people from "cloistered contemplatives to those involved in very active occupations" (which includes me) benefit from delving into the *Rule* (Barry, p. 41). It is imperative to my continued health – emotional, physical and spiritual – that I strive for **acceptance** in each day's march. It ties in well with Benedict's emphasis on obedience. Yet we know that life, cloistered or not, is a journey with occasional detours we would prefer not to take. I hope that as you read on, you will find inspiration to create a deeper faith in God's love for you, where ever you may roam.

Since Alcoholics Anonymous cautions us to be humble in matters of "press, radio and films," I will cast a wide net when gathering my fellow recovering members in for acknowledgment. I am grateful for the support of Roger F., Nancy A., Kim T., Donna S., and Ruth & Leon J. Group W-32's members and leadership changed throughout the years, so I simply thank all of our trusted servants from 1989 to the present. And I thank Matt Talbot for his blessed stubbornness, the little Irish drunk who found the amazing grace to die as a respected and sober man.

A fresh dilemma! Fr. Bill Guerard and his whole family led us out of the desert right to Jordan's shore. But where to start acknowledging the scores of others who joyfully bear the yoke of pastoral ministry, and those who stand at their sides? I met so many from all over the world with various callings: Benedictine and Franciscan Brothers, priests, deacons, bishops, lawyers, missionaries, and just ordinary, devoted people. There was tremendous joyful sacrifice all around. People opened their churches and offices for meetings, they traveled to educate our parish, they hosted retreats, they set out coffee and cake, they nervously drove at night, they joined in prayer regardless of the circumstance, gave up hours for business meetings, all doing the best they could. May God bless them all – I don't want to leave anybody out by naming some. The parish of St. George's Helmetta must also be acknowledged for its faithfulness in both their Lord and their leadership. Nothing went perfectly but we made great allowances for each other, and that was enough.

I have found true friends on this parallel journey. When I reflect on where I came from, and where God has taken me, I find much for which to be grateful. And so I also thank my parents, Thomas Patrick (may he rest in Peace) and Anne, who set me on the right path. Eventually, I found it again.

INTRODUCTION

If I may again highlight the one point that set this little book into motion, it was *acceptance*. It is a quality required of people who want a Higher Power to guide their lives and expand their hearts. Unfortunately, humanity's nature does not favor acceptance but instead seeks control. You will find a common striving for acceptance among those in recovery from all sorts of addictions, battling self-will run riot. But you will also find it among fairly ordinary people aiming to know God better day by day. With my own particular Christian orientation, God is the mysterious Trinity of Father, Son and Holy Spirit. Deepening this faith led me to attend spiritual retreats crafted for alcoholics. I attended my first Matt Talbot retreat in 1989 to find a Benedictine community's hospitality. A love of reading led me to learn more about St. Benedict and the monastic life. If you learn about Benedict of Nursia, you learn about the *Rule*. Benedict was born in the 5th century and made it nearly halfway into the sixth. He founded the monastic community of Monte Cassino where he was its first Abbot.

Once a man pledged to enter the monastery for good, his life was willingly given over to the rule of the Abbot in charge. It intrigued me to learn that after his vow, no "Brother" was allowed to venture out beyond the walls, unless sent on a specific journey by the Abbot. Such permission was infrequently granted, usually involving a special task or mission well-suited to that man. One chapter of the *Rule* (RB 67) is entitled: *Brothers Sent on a Journey*. My first little paperback translation of RB 67 ends with this admonition: "Anyone who leaves the monastery, goes anywhere, or does anything, however small, without the Abbot's permission will be punished."

Well, it turned out that God – my Abbot – had some journeys in mind for me and not a few others. The retreat house hosting my home group was closing. Our final gathering was in January of 2001, starting Matt Talbot Group W32's journey. We thought we would be there until time wound up, and could think of no other place to compare with our beautiful Queen of Peace. It would take a miracle!

In 2003, the Episcopal Church of the USA broke away from Anglican and Christian tradition, fueled by the impatience of a minority faction that was not getting its way. A majority vote at a Convocation of the U.S. Bishops cast aside official and emotional warnings from "across the pond" in Canterbury, England, and consented to ordain Gene Robinson, an openly homosexual man, as the Bishop of New Hampshire. It's very (very) important that you are aware that this was meant to be a huge distraction. While this was the lightening rod issue, my parish was being made aware of deeper concerns.

We saw an accelerating rejection of Biblical authority, the dismissal of sin, salvation and repentance, and wholesale adoption of a disastrous, feel-good way of "doing church." The combination of eroding foundations, shocking developments and Robinson's ordination would (and does to this day) result in many laypeople, and even whole Dioceses, praying for an answer. For some, the decision was to come apart from the Episcopal Church of the USA [ECUSA]. But it was usually at the cost of their buildings and assets, the bringing of lawsuits, and being locked out with no prior warning. This was the possibility that my priest and parish friends were facing. Would we be cast out, too? Would our lovely church in Helmetta stand empty for the first time since 1893 for the sake of a political agenda? And so, this was the second journey: our mental and physical preparations to leave, while praying and waiting on God, still hoping with all our might to stay. That seemed like a big request, but we knew God was in the miracle business.

Getting back to St. Paul's Abbey, the fate of the rest of their property across the road from the Queen of Peace was less dire. The school remained active, as did the chapel. The remaining men and a few women there carry on their various occupations. Later, Korean leaders revived St. Paul's mission to educate men for missionary work here or back overseas. The sweet little gift shop is still open, packed to the rafters with all that such a place should properly have to offer. People from the area will hopefully still worship in the chapel, and come to enjoy the ritual of solemn prayer and plainsong offered throughout the day. I suppose there is still an Alcoholics Anonymous meeting, since little more is needed for that than a few chairs and a coffeepot.

Some of the expenses of St. Paul's were covered by the annual sale of Christmas trees. Following the tradition of a monastery providing for its own support, a good deal of the property was devoted to tree-raising. For many customers, the winter journey to select and cut their tree was a family tradition; people came from near and far. In the few weeks before Christmas Day, the fragrant green fields were jolted by movement and the nearly-constant grinding sound of the tree baler. Barking dogs and laughing children of several families raced around, while the adults moved slowly up and down the rows, sizing up the crop of evergreens. They would call in the children for the final selection, carry it in triumph to the baler line and settle accounts. With the bundled prize tied securely and accounts settled, they began their drive home. Some journeys, like the tree search, are short and purposeful beginnings of prolonged celebration. My two journeys took a lot longer!

For the women of Matt Talbot Movement Retreat Group W-32, the "Abbot" *we* served was *the God of our understanding*, as A.A. describes a Higher Power. For the parish of St. George's Church, the head of our house was Jesus Christ. So I write this book from the perspective held by a recovering alcoholic Christian, a servant of the Father, Son and Holy Spirit, responsible for carrying A.A.'s message to others. I am a person of place, one who may *be* moved but does not internally complete the process until the Holy Spirit comes and blesses the new place or the new understanding.

I describe the Abbey and the Queen of Peace Retreat House with the detail that God allowed me to see and remember over several years and with the feelings granted over time. These feelings – sorrow, joy, wonder, redemption, denial, anger, and acceptance – are some of the riches and treasures of sobriety. As drunks, we feel little and prefer that numb emptiness. Even while writing this introduction, finally getting to publication in late 2012, tears sting my eyes as gratitude fills my heart. Amazing Grace, how sweet the sound, that saved a wretch like me!

As for that parish…well, I'll fill you in on their milestones along the way too, since both these journeys are interwoven. I relate my tales from the perspective of being a member, and in some years part of the Vestry of St. George's Church. The responsibility for the financial and other matters of a parish can be a challenge in ordinary times, but our group had a lot more on the "to-do list" for several years.

Both groups were (and are) held gently in God's hand. May you use the example of our acceptance of "the Abbot's" orders to soften the inevitable changes in your own life's journey. Go forth, and fear not!

CHAPTER ONE

The Trailhead of Each Journey

*Those who are sent on a journey should commend themselves
to the prayers of all the community as well as the superior
and, at the last prayer at the work of God in the oratory, there
should always be a memento of all who may be absent.*

_RB 67.1

St. George's Anglican Church, Helmetta, New Jersey

In the fickle New Jersey springtime of 2005, I contemplated how like God it was to use somebody like me to help guide a church in a time of crisis. Was He an apprentice, picking up any tool on the bench for such a delicate task? No. Unsure of my own ability as I was, I knew His hand could never fall amiss, and so had agreed to serve St. George's as part of the leadership.

This was not an ordained position, merely an elected one, but it did require an anointing. We all were blessed for duty - the new Vestry members, the Junior Warden and me as incoming Warden - with a firm swipe of fragrant ointment on hands and forehead to commission us as we stood before our congregation. We were now officially part of the group of twelve that would serve our respective terms. It was a routine ritual, nonetheless it linked us with the ghosts of those who had served before. Our denomination is sometimes called one of the "high" churches, but frankly many of us were feeling quite low. The ECUSA had been behaving badly for years and showed no sign of turning back. They wanted to create a whole "new thing" without much definition offered aside from newness. It was a baffling, embarrassing and volatile period, difficult to accept or explain.

I was surfing the 'net early one morning, hoping to learn the fate of a priest I had been reading about in the newspaper. He served an Episcopal church up in Connecticut, a man I'd never met, but I wanted to see if God had another bit of data for me to consider. I could hardly believe that I was Warden of a Vestry that might be called upon to commit treason in the eyes of certain bishops: we wanted to hold fast to tradition, Scripture, and reason. It seemed unreal. Would we decide to shake off the dust of ECUSA and take shelter under the broader wing of Anglicanism? Or would we remain, and thereby lend silent assent to what our own priest saw as a mass death march down a wide, smooth highway to hell?

Rising from my chair, bearing my still warm but empty coffee cup to the kitchen for a refill, some inane lyrics from an old AC/DC song attached to that last thought. "H*iiiighway to HELL!* da da da DA da da da da...*hiiighway to HELL!*" Humor helps! A lot of people in the parish seemed to be in deep denial, more anxious about a proposed piece of artwork over the altar than by a pending denominational split. Actually, that made sense. The artwork being offered was an issue that we could evaluate and resolve with discussion. This much larger, menacing controversy sounded like the threat of dragons in the sea on ancient maps. What did it have to do with "our" Sundays? We came into our lovely old church, sang the cherished old hymns, heard a solid, convicting sermon and exchanged the Peace – could all this nastiness be real? They weren't apathetic, just bewildered by the speed of decay in a fabric they had always assumed was heavy canvas, turning out to be cheesecloth.

My lazy dialup connection has been chugging away and so I return with more coffee to find plenty of references for one Rev. Christopher Leighton. Now, it's not that I know all these priests by name or anything. But I have a folded quarter page of newsprint from April 29, 2005 and that's all that you need these days to snoop anybody's life. The article has a photo, and I superstitiously avoid it when setting down my cup. He looks like a great guy, this Fr. Christopher, about the same age as our priest Fr. Bill Guerard, that firm swiper of holy ointment across my hands and forehead. The picture shows him in his office, and I imagine there the peculiar scents of a church: the trace of old Easter incense, healing ointment, beeswax, and furniture polish. In the picture, an impressive grouping of crosses adorns the wall, and Rev. Leighton is holding one before the interviewer, the chain in his right hand and the cross in his left. The fully extended chain is alive with captured motion, and shimmers like the Holy Spirit moving from God's hand to a newly-minted planet, shocking the whole thing alive.

The Reverend has nice hands. Strong and capable, long fingers and an artful way of elevating the little cross as he tells its story. And suddenly, I am in Newton, New Jersey, brought back in my very Spirit to what I called the "Rock of Crosses." I let the full memory take shape.

3

Sitting on a frail wooden bench, a bit of snow falling in the fading light of a January Saturday evening. Out the corner of my eye I see deer moving to their feeding places, but the Rock commands my attention. Birds are tucking in, cheeping little blessings of *Goodnight!* to one another. Now all around is nearly silent in this place where God waits to draw in and minister to the seeker. So rare, velvet draped, this quiet. It is achingly beautiful, the communion of the Spirit and the Created.

> Have I not commanded you? Be strong and of good courage;
> be not frightened, neither be dismayed; for the Lord your
> God is with you wherever you go. (Joshua 1:9)

It will be in that same kind of quiet assurance for me and our priest, Vestry and parish, to choose what we will do, knowing little more than Whom we follow. I blink, returning to the present, and find myself thinking of my first Holy Communion in May of 1956. I shake my head in wonder that my painfully memorized Catechism was being morphed into "hate speech" by tragic and foolish liberal interpretation. I bookmark a few references for later on and log off. It is time to go to work, time to pray again on the way, to see if this is the day the Abbot of my soul will instruct me. Turns out, I must continue to wait and watch for a number of years. So let me tell you about the wonderful women, the monks, and our Queen of Peace to start the second journey's tale.

**St. Paul's Abbey and the Lovely Queen
of Peace, a House of Welcome**

*The greatest care should be taken to give a warm reception to the poor and
to pilgrims, because it is in them above all others that Christ is welcomed.*

_RB 53.4

Newton, New Jersey. It was the town nearest to the Abbey, so we just said "Newton" when asked where Group W-32's Retreat was held. Newton is indeed a city on a hill, Jerusalem to the Abbey, since you went *up* to reach its rural magnificence. Big stone buildings around the town square, statues to honor their not-forgotten heroes, all of the small town icons. You could find some stunning Victorian mansions up there. These had never been let go to seed like those Painted Ladies down in Cape May. Ever seeing, these grand homes sat high and securely on lush landscaped pedestals, history drifting past their awning-hooded eyes.

Newton even had an A.A. clubhouse, relatively rare to find, and a terrific Army/Navy store. Normally, such conditions would have drawn many in our particular group of women like the hand of an old friend. But if you hooked up with W-32, it might be years before you even considered going to town. The monastic pull, a spiritual gravity, kept us close to the House and the grounds. People in recovery programs often have a tendency to substitute motion or urgency for contemplation and quiet. Here, it all changed once your duffel hit the floor of your room. We came to *stay*, regardless of the pain of healing, regardless of how long it took to happen, or at what hour.

During the long free time on Saturday, those of us not journaling, isolating, talking, crying or sleeping departed the building as one (noisy, loud) group but later would split into two: the Shoppers and the Walkers. We bunched up for safety to sprint across Rt. 206, a two-lane speedway with a tricky curve. Once across, *Shoppers* headed for the Abbey's gift shop, peeling off to the left, steps quickening. There was something about being in the Abbey that tended to calm, but not quench, the shopping mania. Here, only "spiritual" purchases could fill the shopping basket, which seemed to mollify any potential guilt. Or you could always just lie and say it was for somebody else, knowing there would be an opportunity for Confession in a few hours.

Walkers kept going, up the hard pack gravel road. There was an old drawing tacked up on the Abbey's main bulletin board that showed a large pond. It was surrounded by a nice, uncomplicated loop road that let the feet do their job, since the unburdening of a soul makes for difficult enough terrain. I was up there twelve years and had never even seen the pond. Once I found the Rock of Crosses around back of the retreat house, I had my pathway and my place of release, not many paces from the back door.

The purpose of Retreat was to get made right again, so you could deal with the coming year of becoming yourself. You see, everything we needed was right there. Nobody *needed* to go into town. Nobody *cared* that our time slot was right after New Year's Day, in the iron cold January of northern New Jersey. That was how you knew you had a good retreat house. But the Abbey was the <u>best</u>. Unquestionably holy, a place dedicated to the Glory of God, even if a blow dryer could cripple the entire electrical system. We were being hosted by a monastic community of Benedictine brothers, men whose lives probably made no sense to somebody living in a Victorian mansion in Newton, and they didn't know the half of it.

The hours we all spent with each other over the years brought us face-to-face with the Father, taught us the humility of Christ, and caught us up in the wild, joyous power of the Holy Spirit. For it was in obedience to that ancient law of hospitality at their last Passover meal together that Jesus was moved to wash the feet of his chastened Disciples (John 13:12). "Do you know what I have done to you?" He asked them afterward. They did not but soon would know that humility was not an option, and neither was Love. Benedict saw *obedience* as the foundation, the master virtue leading to higher and higher levels of humility.

The Queen of Peace was closed to retreat guests in 2001, leaving memory as our only way of return. But this can be the best way to recall what we've loved. We would only be trespassers in a condemned building, not pilgrims welcomed into warmth. Yet, since I was granted permission to take some pictures in December of 2006, we must admit that St. Paul's is still a place of welcome. And the gift shop remains open!

CHAPTER 2

The Welcome of St. Paul's Abbey

Guidelines for Christian and Monastic Good Practice ...
to love your neighbor as much as you love yourself.

_RB Chapter 4.1

The House: Queen of Peace

St. Paul's Abbey was blessed with a large and gracious retreat house. All long rectangles and arched doorways, with wide iron staircases that connected the few floors, and huge heavy stone walls: a very castle. That such an imposing stone structure could contain our snug harbor was a miracle falling just short of the Incarnation. Some women gave a heaving sigh of relief as they made their way through the little group of smokers near the back door's threshold. Carefully stuffed bags of luggage fell forgotten to the foyer floor to leave arms free for enfolding friends. Guest rooms were on all floors, the few on the ground floor being for the women with mobility challenges. All others were on the second and third floors. A small sitting room on the ground floor served as the check-in station, and a (noisy, loud) *Welcome!* hung in the air and rang off the walls.

With the monks' famous ability to hover attentively while remaining politely detached, you needed to tune in to feel their presence. You had to learn which of the barely-open doors was Fr. Andrew's counsel room, so your educated glance met a crackling blue Irish eye with its rays of laugh lines. Nodding and winking back, properly blessed in, I could turn my attention to the "new fish" I had brought, and herd them through the registration process.

"Give your money to her…here's a name tag…what? Oh, that's the God Box…don't worry, they'll tell you later. OK, lots of time, let's get our stuff upstairs. No, there is no elevator. Mush!"

The energy of women released from routine and actually expected to indulge their constant craving for rest created updrafts and spirals of conflicting emotions and reactions. And yet, it was obvious to all that the place was meant for retreating from life's clamor. It was a good and safe place. This sturdy, overarching calm compacted the energy and untangled each new knot of arrivals, as they went off to find their rooms.

The Rooms

Avoid all pride and self-importance

_RB 4.5

Each room had a number, and some doors also bore little brass "In Memory of…" plaques, a reminder that we are dust, and to dust we shall return. The standard was that if a door stood open and nothing on the bed, the room was free for the taking. There was no point looking into neighboring rooms to compare; rooms were set up for one or for a few but that was the only difference. Whether one found the simple furnishings adequate or shockingly sparse depended upon the degree of humility attained.

You got a narrow bed, a narrow closet, a small desk with a wooden chair & small lamp. There was usually a sink with a medicine cabinet over and a thin metal towel rack. The rooms were too cold unless they were too hot. On top of the desk would be a Bible and a paper copy of the house rules encased in a clear but yellowed vinyl sleeve with an oilcloth border stitched all around. Sometimes you'd find an ancient cigarette burn on a desk edge or a window sill, signs of the past before smoke alarms sniffed and shrilled.

The Veterans come well supplied with two pens, spiral notebook or maybe a journal, heavy duty PJ's, robe, towels and not much else. Maybe their own coffee cup if they had been hippies earlier in life, plus something possibly homemade for the snack table.

Newcomers begin unpacking their bulging duffels and start nesting. They heap or carefully position various objects of a decidedly impractical nature all over their rooms. Typically observed in this ritual activity are large to micro-sized stuffed animals, candles that cannot be lit due to fire hazard, and clothing fit for three days in any season. These bare necessities are followed by stacks of books, color-coded journals, snacks, *extra* snacks and a disturbing array of personal care items. Sometimes there was still the need for a shampoo run by Saturday. Their snack offerings ranged from vegan-compliant mysteries to boxes of huge glazed donuts. In the room of the Newcomer, St. Benedict's assertion that private ownership of objects was a practice to be uprooted (RB 33) met its opposite determination – to personalize, to declare: "This is ME! Well, so far…"

The One Warning to All

Keep the reality of death always before your eyes

_RB 4.7

Veterans must watch lest a Newcomer withdraw from bag or case the one truly forbidden object, the electric blow dryer, in order to apply immediate correction. It will be oft repeated. As the nerves of the human body are designed to process only so much stress, the thin, fragile electrical system of the House would simply collapse from the ravenous drain of power. This is the one object of which the monks solemnly warn the retreatants at the common opening session on Friday. It is an instrument of the devil, born of vanity (they never *said* that but it was clear).

We are finally impressed into compliance by the news that the *coffee pots* will be affected, and a murmur of resolve finally moves among the women. (I wonder who will be the one to learn that a curling iron can do the same thing. As ever, man-woman communication eludes us.) Along with the hair dryer warning, we are told that we must "be nice" to the Bell Ringer. Indeed, it is even printed on our schedule sheet! She has been assigned a noble task and is not to be cajoled into skipping any part of the House as she tolls an alert before each event. She is not to be threatened with death by now-useless hair dryer cord, regardless of the strength of that urge. *Sober women are self-controlled.*

We are even more impressed that the monks continue to observe the ancient instrument RB 4.1 …*not to kill,* when someone on the third floor fires up a hair dryer at 6:30 a.m., giving the old House another nervous breakdown. Coffee is a bit late that morning, and so the name of the offender is not released. This is due to the wisdom of the Brothers, gleaned from their Biblical lessons on the nature of mob rule. Once was enough.

Our Brothers, Our Selves

These [monks] are the ones who are based in a monastery and fulfill
their service of the Lord under the rule of an abbot or abbess.

_RB 1.1

A particular challenge to about 100 women on retreat would seem to be the nearly constant proximity of men, but even the most wanton and base among us recognized the "Brothers" as a special type, not to be trifled with…pretty much. Occasional reminders were helpful: *sober women are self-controlled*. Some of the Brothers were also recovering alcoholics and with their duty to interact with retreatants, actions that would have nonplussed ol' St. Benedict abounded here. Hugs, for example, are part of the currency of recovery and the exchange rate was high at the Abbey. These are my descriptions of a few of our friends, to which you are welcome to add if you knew them, too. Go ahead, scribble or draw in the margins (with apology to you e-book readers!)

Brother Andrew

Listen, child of God, to the guidance of your teacher.

_Prologue 1

I mentioned briefly Bro. Andrew and will now gladly expand the memory. Tall, with rugged face, piercing blue eyes, and abundant silver hair swept back. Andrew clearly enjoyed being just where he had been placed by God. But there was much in the way he carried himself that showed traces of his plowing through life as a drunk. He had the easy grace of the old barroom, the place of early welcome, our sanctuary and then nearly our tomb in the darker days. You could tell that his past "drunkdom" had been lived full tilt, take no prisoners, yes it's misery but it's <u>my</u> misery! The worse we were, the more glory to God for the way we are: that was Andrew.

In private counsel, Bro. Andrew's way was to draw out your dreams rather than to add advice. He helped you see that your heart's desires were not all that far off, but that much work lay in between. I can still hear his voice urging me on when things get tough, the wind at my back. He emphasized the very practical nature of a holy (set apart for a purpose) life, reflecting the Prologue's further assertion: "It is not easy to accept and persevere in obedience, but it is the way to return to Christ, when you have strayed through the laxity and carelessness of disobedience." Andrew, I'll see you on the other side. Have a good 24! [1]

---

1   A common parting expression among some A.A.'s, relating to the 24 hours in a single day.

Brother Joel

Don't be lazy nor give way to excessive sleep.

_RB 4.5

The women assemble at the scheduled time in the second-floor Chapel, talking as they must, albeit in somewhat hushed tones at this early hour. Most are not even aware that Bro. Joel in his dark brown robe is occupying a space near the little altar. In a human imitation of the very dawn, Joel silently radiates some kind of monkish energy that causes eyes to suddenly glance his way. This sets off a chain reaction of elbows poking neighboring sides and a faint sound like incoming surf, a long "Shhhhh…" Time for something to begin, Newcomers perceive, and give a final, settling-in wriggle of the tush in their plastic seats.

Brother Joel is the light-bringer. It is his particular, quiet joy to teach us about the Light. Through Joel's calm and leading voice, we learn to marvel at the mysterious power of light. He brings us to the start of an awareness of a deeper, Spirit-fed Light within…within us! Lousy, bitchy unworthy souls that we may seem to ourselves, the Light does not care. It will not do anything less than cleanse, soothe and uplift if offered a simple invitation. Would we open heart and mind? That simple question will be pondered over the weekend. Without saying the actual name, Joel conveys the Holy Spirit's constant presence just by the awe in his voice when he speaks of light. He seemed permanent as the chapel walls, awaiting another dawn to replace another sunset.

But then, much like the light of a long summer's evening, he was suddenly gone! Joel was in Africa, Bro. Basil told us one year as we arrived. I sorrowed at first, but then held an image in my mind of a brilliant dot of light coming to rest someplace in the Dark Continent, spreading outward, silently brushing back the misery of famine, AIDS, malaria and dying children, joyfully illuminating the land from that central force -- Joel's simple, beautiful faith. They needed it more than we did, I guess.

Brother Justin – "the Drunk Monk"

…guarding against the subtle danger of excessive
drinking leading to drunkenness. _RB 40.2

You get all kinds in A.A. One of the resident brothers would at times be our retreat leader, and so would tell his story as part of his opening talk on Friday night. Bro. Justin would raise an eyebrow and ask us at various points, "What do you do…with a drunk monk?" Indeed, few around him back in the day knew the answer to that question. The local police, his fellow brothers, the Abbot – all would periodically clash with the peculiar, baffling nature of the disease of alcoholism. Finally, Justin found the fellowship of A.A., a host of people who knew <u>exactly</u> what to do with a drunk anybody.

Bro. Justin was relatively young and was often described by Newcomers as "cute" – a term that always set off a Roman Catholic reflex of ducking from lightning bolts if I was nearby. He delighted us with tales of hiding bottles in the surprisingly designed monk's robe with its deep pockets. He drew us into his pain of the many repeated failures, like our own. He had us nodding heads as we women completely identified with his obsessive schemes to get that next drink. But now he was sober, redeemed and serving God rather than himself. Clearly, it was working just fine for all concerned.

A while back I heard he had died. Cancer. But we will see him again – with all of our Brothers! – at the end of the age, and it will be wonderful.

CHAPTER 3

Pillar of Fire, Pillar of Cloud: The Little Church on the Hill… Waits

*Even the sparrow finds a home, and the swallow a
nest for herself where she may lay her young, at thy
altars, O Lord of hosts, my King and my God.*

_Psalm 84:3

Our priest, Fr. Bill Guerard, knew the game was over long before most parish members were willing to believe that things were "that bad." *Bad* meant being suddenly pushed out of our church building, our assets seized, our records hauled out of the office, and the doors padlocked. Normally our entry doors were not locked, to provide a place of refuge and prayer regardless of the hour, so the image was disturbing. Of the theological affairs most people expressed concern, but it seemed like high-level stuff that would eventually settle out. Hadn't it always? For a handful of others who faithfully followed these events, along with Fr. Bill and those who served on Vestry, the theological issues were the most huge and the most heartbreaking.

Institutions could come and go, buildings could be restored, but now the 1970's had come home to roost. A "new thing" was being relentlessly promoted and praised by the liberal hordes. We listened in vain for their definition of what the new thing meant. It was the sort of catchy phrase that tingled in the ear, tantalized the mind, and could easily be thrown like a blanket to smother conservative objections like ours. They were the new, we were the old.

The parade to perdition was chronicled on several websites, with David Virtue's being the most thorough. I read there the odd news of "womens' liturgies" that clicked and dragged Wiccan overlays of worship into the sanctioned practices of the Book of Common Prayer. There were gay union blessings, baptisms of what I call "ta-da!" babies: children engineered as if ordering a new car with certain options. There was adultery, gossip barbed with anger, the robbing God of tithes and offerings, and worse of all, *murmurings*! Now, you might not think complaining undertones aren't so bad in comparison, but Benedict has many warnings against it, so let's take a lesson. Overall, a lot of crazy and unacceptable behavior had crept into God's family, and so the family was fracturing on a worldwide scale. The armor now belonged to the Anglicans across the seas and beneath the equator. The Holy Spirit was joyfully dancing with the Third World people who were open to miracles and wonders. Many of them had no church building and met where they could, mainly in homes just like the early Church. Their leaders walked to meetings at constant risk of robbery and beatings, some fatal. Yet they went, step by prayerful step.

Something had to give. It all cascaded down with a crash in 2003 with the ordination of Gene Robinson as Bishop of New Hampshire. It was no surprise that ECUSA would try out the waters by nominating and electing an openly gay man. But they had done so in direct rebellion to pleas and directives to hold off on taking action to continue in dialogue and study. Things were just not moving fast enough to suit them, so like spoiled children they threw tantrums and acted out, centuries of tradition be damned.

The icing on the cake followed soon after, the very sudden election of a new Presiding Bishop for ECUSA (ta-da!). She was (and is at this writing) an extremely liberal woman bent on stamping out any resistance on the part of "the minority" of biblically literate and faithful people. She made public statements that went 180 degrees opposite of beliefs that are foundations of the Christian faith. Jesus Christ, for example, was not "the" way to salvation, just a nice option. Sin? Oh, such an old-fashioned concept, very damaging to self-esteem – let's throw that out, too! Those readers who are parents, think a moment: how does *not ever* disciplining a child work out in the long run? That's where all this seemed to be headed.

Not content with trashing ancient tradition and re-working the Bible, our new Presiding Bishop started an aggressive campaign of suing anyone who *dared* dissent. She was especially harsh toward Anglicans overseas that were already offering a refuge for "conservatives," our new label compliments of ECUSA. It was obviously going to be a limited choice: her way, or the road to Perdition.

Our own local bishop, the Rt. Rev. George Councell, was being biblically pastoral in his dealings with us – wonderfully so! I first met Bishop Councell back when he was one of the nominees for the position, and even then he was firmly committed to giving each parish what he called "a place to stand" in the Diocese. He knew there was no unity over the distressing issues raised by livin' in the USA, and that was <u>years</u> before Robinson came on the scene. It was a daring stance, actually.

With respect to our particular situation, we met several times over the years both in his Trenton NJ office and at Helmetta, the whole Vestry or just a few. Each meeting began, ended with and was surrounded by prayer and intercession. Later, we added time for the laying on of hands and healing prayer. Our Bishop had contracted Parkinson's disease and was digging in for a hard fight, so we stood with him in faith. That is how "church" is supposed to work, and it was good. Considering the circumstances.

We all kept in prayer that we would see the Lord's pillars of cloud and fire guiding us along, and we waited. Our Vestry voted to withhold 10% of our financial contribution to the Diocese, directing it elsewhere, as a statement of our dissent. Our Deacon, Greg, remained with us as assigned. The Vestry began to refer to the process as a very slow game of tennis. Bop….return…bop…

Nobody came to kick us out, so we waited some more, doing ministry with quiet, steady purpose. In 2007, we withheld *all* of the contribution. Still no eviction notice, everybody still on board. Rather than become nervous wrecks, we decided to plan for the worst. Spiritual gifts of administration, helps, and vision were deployed. Our members in business knew something about the incredibly detailed process of "becoming" a new legal entity. Those with research skills spent hours finding insurance and workable investment options. Others drove around and assessed other potential gathering places for Sunday worship. All were dealing with some loss of income or members as fear managed to creep in here and there. We officially voted as a parish to join CANA, the Convocation of Anglicans in North America, and *still* no eviction while we continued to meet and negotiate. In early 2008 we made a position for a Youth Minister, and we expanded the Praise Band. More people started visiting, then staying, then getting involved. We were growing!

Oh, the wondrous Cross! By itself, a horrible means of torture and death meted out to the worst of the worst. But redeemed by God, the self-sacrificial death of His only Son transformed the cross into the most enduring symbol of hope, change and new life. We kept on praying, worshipping, watching…and waiting.

CHAPTER 4

Back to Newton: The Rock of Crosses

*The first step of humility is to cherish at all times the sense
of awe with which we should ever turn to God*

_RB 7.4

We cannot always reach the memories we must pull out of our past without some ministry by the Great Physician. Some of us had to be placed before the Rock of Crosses. A visit to this spot would result in a deep and naturally painful spiritual massage. Out of the heart's darkest storehouse came the acidic secrets, the buried memories, the unfaced shame or guilt. The Rock was often found by a restless Walker, meandering along the natural path behind the Guest House that once served the work of the old farm. If one returned the same way and noticed a particular angle hinting at another path to the right, the choice was to ignore or explore. Following the way between oaks and pines, up a little rise and then rounding a bend, the Walker suddenly stops, confused and unsure of protocol.

Confronted by what seemed to be a burial mound, should they continue? To the left, there was an impressive pile of split and whole gray rocks of all sizes, from easy chair to sugar bag, randomly pushed by one of earth's shrugs to about five feet at the high point. The formation looms forbiddingly while at the same time bids you to come even closer. Still feeling a sense of invasion, made sharper once the first cross is glimpsed, you have come far enough to feel one of God's sentry angels take your hand. *The doctor will see you now.* With this permission you willingly move forward, turn left again. The leading stops. You stop. Amazed, you let your eyes wander, in the way a giant must gaze on a village landscape. Yet no planet holds this formation; the rocks *bristle* with crosses!

There is a fantastic array of them to see, but not just *see*; it is willed that you actually *feel* the crafter's hands setting and declaring each particular memorial. And so you are surrounded by a galaxy of emotions. For each cross had to be imagined, fashioned, and infused with some deep sacrifice of the soul. Be it a Godly sorrow, a Godly rejoicing or an intercessor's empathy for the pain of another, it was infused into their cross. Then it would be left there against the raging mountain winds, the rain and ice and the merciful covering of snow. As the seasons passed, some of the offerings would have settled back into the Rock. All that remained was hope.

Without the honest owning of the infused emotion and the sacrifice of self-will this took, no cross could have been attached. No, not one, since The Cross carries the cost of sacrifice, represents a final leaving behind of everything. To be able to express an emotion to the extent that humans are allowed is our Godly distinction. The Rock of Crosses represented a huge, undeniable testimony to the need for us to hit that bottom level of a thing. We can only then admit our single powerlessness, and willingly team up with our Higher Power. Walker or Shopper, holy or heathen, the Rock of Crosses was overwhelming. It was the hidden heart of the alcoholics and others who came to the Abbey…but maybe you never saw it, so I'll describe it now.

Seeing this place for the first time, being exposed to that degree of spiritual power in your softened-up retreat mode, made you instinctively want to pay respect to the life force. A weathered and spindly bench was ready as a catcher for those overcome at a tent meeting, strong enough to take your suddenly sagging body. Amazed, you sit and let your eyes wander over this rustic shrine. There were crosses *everywhere*.

Crosses there are made of wood. Twigs, bound into shape by long strands of grass. Longer, heavier branch sections made into a cross with wire hanger or string. Shards of barn siding nailed once, the cross beam now sliding a bit to one side, not quite an X yet. Carved, ornate crosses of wood meant to be indoors, lovingly bathed in lemon oil and rubbed to a sheen, were out here instead. These had been sacrificed to the Rock, a richer symbol of the cost. If you were an outdoors kind of gal, you could easily imagine how splinters could pierce your hand while you jammed your wooden cross into the place granted you by the angels. You might learn that pain was indeed necessary to growth, but your hand would be wrapped around the Cross. The pain would become a useful tool if you stayed on the road He let you find.

Crosses there are made of metal. Large nails, soldered at the juncture and so perhaps made in advance to bring up the the Abbey. Twisted, heavy wire crosses, some fantastically ornate or folk-art crude, all were compelling. Crosses made from bent pieces of mismatched metals, the heavy holding the lighter beam that twisted around it like a serpent. Manufactured crosses of metal once gracing walls or the tops of caskets, meant to be indoors and protecting all occupants, were out here instead. If you were a nurturing kind of gal, you might ache to cover the unsheltered images of Jesus attached to most of these crosses, but that was never necessary. You might learn that God craves your open heart that He may enter. Indeed, "…he will rejoice over you with gladness, he will renew you in his love; he will exult over you with loud singing as on a day of festival." (Zephaniah 3:17)

Crosses there are made of clay or plaster. These are humble and fragile, but nonetheless given with free will to the Rock. These crosses added touches of color, of softness and surrender. For who could expect one of these to last very long out in the elements? Most were already broken, their pieces fallen step-like according to the configuration of the stones, yet still retaining their shape, always The Cross. If you were an abused kind of gal, you were glad of the mossy old bench so you could just sit and weep for as long as it took to start healing your own broken, shattered heart. Pine boughs nod in encouragement, sweeping away tears to allow even more, to flood the past and overwhelm its now diminished power. You have learned that surrender to being flawed and broken, even faded and shattered, is of little account to the Spirit, who will give you the victory.

Whatever anyone undertakes in the monastery must have the approval of the Abbot.

_RB 49.2

Snow often covered the Rock of Crosses, since W-32 came up in January. If it was deep enough, the snow concealed many of the smaller crosses, or the other objects that people had left behind as an offering. Small frames holding moist, warped pictures, small and large statues staring in whatever direction the animals and weather had moved their heads. Rosary beads were draped over points of rocks or other crosses. A sobriety medallion had been nailed into a rock, creating a particularly disturbing witness. I briefly imagined the sound the fastening would have made, ringing off the rocks and the wall of the House, wondered if the point had been victory or a tragic giving-way.

There are crevices that hold creased and sodden cards, the kind you get at funeral homes with name, dates and a poem on one side, a comforting image on the other. Poking up randomly are artificial flowers, plastic well weathered to a translucent, pastel range of colors. Yet the crosses cannot all be hidden; there are simply too many of them and they preside over the whole area, and not just the mound of rocks. Crosses are lashed to trees, they surround the perimeter of the Rock like sprouts, they hang from branches on fishing line or bakery string, twisting as the angels breathe upon them while they guard and tend the Rock.

As from another world apart I hear voices and laughter drifting from well behind me and to the right, a pack of Shoppers returning from the hunt. Rising and picking a way back through the other side of the rise along the deer path, I move away from the sound to circle around the House to its front entrance. It was too soon for me to be able to share in their joys. My past, like drying mud on shoes, needed to flake off before I could be of any use to my sisters. What happens at the Rock of Crosses, like on the Mount of Transfiguration, stays there. We can carry back only the awe and wonder, but that is certainly more than enough.

CHAPTER 5

Recollections from Ten-Plus Years of Retreats at The Abbey

Traces of the Farm

Daily Manual Labor

_RB 48

Alone Nuthatch, tough little birds that stick to the trunks of trees like Velcro on mesh, makes a jerky, toy-like progression over an old oak to probe the deep crevices in the bark. This one that I can see begins a tootling call to the hidden others. Their tinhorn songs now come from several directions to announce the setting of the sun as I return from a long walk. I have been in the barns, in the equipment sheds, across the bumpy fields and up and down the valleys, poking curiously around like a Nuthatch myself.

I always mourn a farm that lies dormant. Always. I want to take it over, get some plump, shiny draft horses and plow away like an Amish farmer. I love the idea of seeds, waiting for their bursting time, poked into moist earth and covered with expectation. The attitude of the farmer reflects obedience and waiting, what I should be doing as a Christian. Each kind of seed has its unique requirement – the soil that barely covers the lettuce seed must be heaped up to hide that of the corn. Cool weather for the peas and the spinach, summer warmth for the squash, a nip of frost makes the carrot or the Brussels sprout all the sweeter. So we humans, come from common clay, also possess a unique journey planned by God. We look in vain for direction if we compare our selves to another, but may learn if we ask in faith for it, day by day.

Who has more faith than the farmer? In the old monastery, the low walls of heaped stone stretched out to surround the garden, the orchard, the vines and the pastures. Life was to be lived according to the light of the day and the drawing dark of evening. Animals were fed before the men would eat. You watched the weather, you planted, you prayed for harvest. In the autumn you gathered crops like wisdom, carefully storing it by a variety of means. This had to be guarded against tiny invaders. And by the time when the last few carrots and potatoes lay in the bins, if all was well the new growth was starting outside. The pure tonic of spring greens, sprouts of asparagus, the humble dandelion and then the rest in turn, were joyfully collected to grace the dinner plate with God's sure promise of life. It would have been good to have had the farm alive also, but that was the way it was when we were there. So be it.

Setting Control Aside, Honoring the Hours

Mutual Obedience in the Monastery

_RB 71

Most retreats have a schedule, and ours was no different. Some structure was necessary, especially for the new fish, who had trouble winding down and were always asking, "Now what?" Along with routine might go a personal tradition or two. I liked to get out my Group W-32 medallion and start wearing it after I had sent in my registration. This meant wearing it for a couple of months, at least. It had a certain weight to it, and the medallion would slide coolly around under my clothes as a constant reminder. Each one was unique in the number it bore, but identical to all the rest in its design. It was given to you as you came to the end of your first retreat, accompanied by a booklet about Matt

Talbot and at least two hugs from those up front who were calling out the names and handing out the goods. My second ritual – as soon as my clean undies and my asthma stuff were in the drawer and my coat in the closet – was *the putting on of the slippers.* I was now officially "in the House" and took my old hippie cup downstairs for the first of many fillings to catch up with my friends.

Retreats had a basic pattern. You started out on Friday night with the first of several Conferences, with the Retreat Master setting the general theme. Saturday morning's Conference would end with a count-off to sort us into several small groups for discussion and sharing. You kept your group number and met together throughout the whole weekend. Well, that was the intention. You have to remember who you're working with here - shifts between groups were pretty much inevitable. Also, some women were not able to tear away from the octopus of family until Saturday morning and gratefully settled into any group.

The nature, teaching method, sex and disposition of retreat leaders present quite a range of personalities, so let's just leave it at that. God is judge. But our one firm request was that retreat leaders share in recovery from alcohol. Under all the (loud, noisy) chaos, our combined feminine energy and coffee jitters, there really *was* a serious and solemn purpose to our Retreat. It was our primary chance to combine escape from the draining demands of our daily routine to work on our program of recovery. Then we could be of service to others, following the download of the past year's assault to our souls.

This was not easy to accomplish in our state of caffeine intake and with the difficulty of letting things we left at home stay out of our minds. But by Sunday we always saw Mission Accomplished. Simply put, you could say it was all due to the Abbey. Queen of *Peace*, remember? St. Benedict knew how to accomplish this peace among community, but we had only the weekend to do the same thing. A good retreat house is a setting in which all of this can be combined, boiled down and released - the marvelous flavors of a satisfying time of coming away and walking a bit with God.

The Bell Ringer

Signaling the Times for the Work of God

_RB 47

There were few wall clocks in the Abbey, and many of the women would leave their watches behind or deliberately remove them in a practice similar to my slipper tradition. In St. Benedict's day these things were not available but there was a definite schedule to the monastic twenty-four hours nonetheless. *Somebody* had to keep time, and in *Rule* 16 we find instructions for The Day Office which reads, in part: "… let us offer praise to our Creator at Lauds, Prime, Tierce, Sext, None, Vespers and Compline, and in the night let us rise to praise him."

If you mark Prime as "noontime" and then go forward three hours it's Tierce. So you see the day was marked with pauses; the monks left their various occupations to assemble. Benedict provided detailed instructions on the songs, psalms and other prayers that made up the framework of a typical monk's day. Some depended on how large the monastery was, since the intention was to honor God with excellence, not simply to observe a schedule and carry out duties. For example, if there was a large population of monks, the arrangement of songs could be more complex.

We on retreat had a schedule, too, with certain "duties" to fulfill (or worm out of), and our means of keeping time took its cue from the way the monks did it – we had a Bell Ringer. This office was typically foisted upon a Newcomer who was blissfully clueless and could be pressed into this service by our calling it an honor. In its way, it *was* an honor, but it also required the Bell Ringer to serve the group faithfully. While having some brief notice of a pending duty would have been helpful to a monk who might be elbow-deep in the laundry tub, for us I suppose it was most helpful to smokers. Our modern shallowness aside, the ringing of the bell also called those of us who were actually "retreating" to attention. Thus warned, one could decide whether or not to detach from their current occupation to attend something else. Generally the decision would come up *yes* for meals, *maybe* if it meant an interruption of our journaling or listening to another, and perhaps a *not happening* if a naptime or a hot bath was at stake.

And so it was that a young maiden would pace bravely up and down each hallway ringing a brass (noisy, loud) bell that somehow translated the mood of the servant as it clanged away. A Bell Ringer who had accepted her fate calmly, with that sense of honor, would deliver a nice regular *ding-ding-ding* as she went along.

The less-enthused might move at a faster pace to get the thing over with, sounding an irregular pattern of dings and stopping short of the hall's end. And the occasional disgruntled Bell Ringer, shocked and resentful at learning the demands of the job, got her revenge on the whole House at the crack of dawn with a tormenting, random *DING-doING-dingggg-**DING**!!* These would also tend to move very slowly, ringing most furiously when passing the rooms of those responsible for her selection.

Before each item on our schedule, the Bell Ringer was supposed to be about five minutes ahead of the curve, pacing through the house, ringing into every corner and hallway. It was impressive that even the most bitter would carry out their task faithfully, a small miracle considering everything that drunkenness meant. From lives hemmed in by desperate cravings, recovering people were released into a strange new world of *choices*. You had to admire and support the Bell Ringer, even without the little reminder to do so that was printed at the bottom of our schedules. This was easy if you began with a kernel of gratitude: *Hey, at least it's not ME*!

Another of W-32's customs: we thanked the Bell Ringer with a small gift on the last day; it was always the same shape but would differ in appearance. And the customary response was always the same shape, too. A bell received…and a smile returned. All was forgiven in the higher realm of acceptance and tolerance that serving others always produced.

The Kitchen Crew

The Fair Provision for the Needs of All -
Qualities Required by the Cellarer

_RB 34

Some of those "flavors"of the retreat were literal. St. Benedict's direction of the necessary operations of a monastery can be found in the *Rule* along with all the holy stuff. Certain staff such as the Cellarer are described, and I noted that one of his qualifications was "sober." Cool. Depending on the size of the cloister, it was directed that he have enough assistants to carry out the necessary functions of supply and distribution.

At times, the Cellarer would not be able to meet a request. St. Benedict similarly instructed the empty-handed Cellarer that "…his response should be a good word for, 'A good word is better than the best gift.' (Eccles. 18:17)." There was no shame in his not having, for apparently <u>God</u> had withheld the item from the Cellarer, and God's will was to be accepted. This is the essence of the "humility" that Benedict associates with the Cellarer. If a request had to be refused, the asker was to respond in kind, with a good word for the Brother who was simply doing his best that day.

This focus on the common physical needs of those in the monastery is of course reflected by our internal capacity when a request comes our way. If we would be wise women, we would have to learn to keep *ourselves* well-supplied, again to meet the needs of others. That action was what kept one "in God's will." What an amazing, simple exchange, rooted in the truth that we have only two things to give: our time and our selves!

As drunks, we spent our *time* in caressing the everfull glass, while looking for the next so the horror of an empty glass would never materialize. Our *selves*, we had simply wasted. Here at the Abbey we would learn how to push the world backward like Superman and redeem the lost years. RB 31.3 includes this instruction: "The members of the community should receive their allotted food without any self-important fuss…" Alas, W-32 members were not always able to adhere to this instruction, since "self-important fuss" was part of the burden of recovery. The Kitchen Crew was often approached with painfully specific dietary requests or had to gently shoo away the self-appointed coffee pot tenders. These were manifestations of the alcoholic obsession with having more than enough. We were always grateful (by Sunday) for the expertise of the Kitchen Crew and the Brothers, who constantly looked over our faults to see God's work in progress behind them.

But we did not leave a lopsided bargain! On the Saturday night of retreat, we had our own A.A. Speakers' meeting, and took up a collection for the group of humble, capable men and women who presented us with lavish meals, hot coffee and the love inherent in hospitality. They did all things well.

I love to remember that long rectangular dining hall with its deeply carved and paneled wooden ceiling and prayers painted on the beige plaster walls. You could see part of the old farm from there, and many mornings the deep stone window sills were mounded with snow, and the weeds beautifully encased in ice.

Matt Talbot's Story

The Abbot's Care of the Excommunicated

_RB 27

Our W-32 group was only one of many devoted to the Matt Talbot Retreat Movement, which is comprised of groups for men, women, and couples. Its central inspiration on earth was a humble Irish drunk who had found sobriety long before A.A. in America was even an idea.

Dirty ol' Dublin was Matt's home and in that city he was but another problem for somebody on any given day. He had found the drink early in his first job at a brewery. His age at the time…well, we would have termed him a "tween." Alcohol remained a constant and growing menace in Matt's life, disguised as a comfort and reward at the work day's end.

He had been making his way in the world, considering, but then one fateful day he ran into some foul luck. No money for the drink he now <u>had</u> to have. But Matt was not too concerned. After all, had he not bought many a round in the pub? Surely one of his own would do the same; he'd be fine after a drink!

But not one person stopped to even say Hello, let alone spring for the price of a drink. This was *very* odd, given the nature of Irish hospitality. So along with his perhaps prideful "taking the pledge" that very day to abstain from alcohol, Matt had to face the brutal process of withdrawal. It was a perfect example of the kind of stupid revenge we alcoholics dream up: "I'll show <u>them</u>! I'll kill <u>me</u>!" Yet Matt hung in there, grimly plowing through each long day with the awful, untreated sickness of alcoholism grinding his guts, pounding his head and twisting his nerves. This is what God gives us to use as a tool against the temptation of drink.

He had always been a good worker, considering, but this time of torment took nearly all the strength he had. So he began stopping into the always-open Catholic church in his neighborhood, just to rest on the way to work, and again on the way home. That turned into times of rest *and prayer*, and then into having conversations with the curious priest (people did not usually linger daily in the church). Soon Matt began taking Holy Communion every day – also not the expected custom of that time. Most Irish then received the Sacrament once a week, some only on special holy days. This was considered a reverent, not neglectful, behavior by the Irish.

Thus it was that the priest got to know Matt and his peculiar mission. After a while Matt was offered books to borrow, which he treasured and treated like gold. Matt renewed his "pledge" for another 90 days, his work became even better and after not too long a time he had all of his very simple needs supplied. Actually, he went well beyond simple, deciding to pattern his life on that of early Irish monks. He became able to take care of his mother, bringing her into his small home. Matt never denied anybody who wanted to borrow money, and so forgave many a debt; he would ask only once for repayment. Self-denial, the polar opposite of the alcoholic's mentality, gradually became a spiritual discipline for Matt. His room, his meals, and his ways all revolved around his relationship with God. Matt also honored the Virgin Mary, as was customary in his religion.

This devotion was revealed when Matt reached his last day on earth. It was a common practice of those who so loved Mary to wear a little chain, like a bracelet, to symbolize their joyful "slavery" to her own life of obedience and humility. But Matt's practice was a tad more extreme (which always gets a knowing laugh from us). He had added some fine metal chains across the torso that were a constant – and probably sometimes pinchy – reminder of who should come first in Matt's life. On that day, his heart gave out suddenly and he did not have a chance to discreetly remove the devotional chains, so they were discovered by the hospital staff that tended the body.

It must have been a touching sight. Perhaps you have heard that the chains were rusted and imbedded in the flesh, but this is a misguided rumor and I welcome the chance to squelch it here. Even after death, Matt Talbot's message was plain: serve and honor God and keep yourself under control. He is buried in Dublin, and some of his simple possessions can still be viewed.

When I would put on my own medallion with its chain in anticipation of the retreat, I thought of Matt. Often the chain was cold, or it pulled out a hair – the tiny pains could generate gratitude that recovery had stopped the huge pains of alcoholism. One year at the Abbey's gift shop, I found a plastic case with little drawers, one for each of the saints. The drawers contained little ovals of metal for attaching to a chain or bracelet, with a raised image of the saint on the front, and a message on the back. While Matt has not yet been granted that degree of honor by the Roman Catholic Church, he is "Venerated." I was pleased to see he had a medal, too, and bought one to attach to my retreat medallion chain. On the back it reads: *Self-control and Charity are sorely needed today.* Amen!

The Chapel Across the Road

Sunday is the day on which all should be occupied in lectio divina,

except for those who are assigned to particular duties.

_RB 48.6

Christmas had passed when we were scheduled to come up. But the celebration of the Epiphany followed, and those who so desired could join the regular Sunday congregation across the street. My first year, I was surprised that people from town came to worship with the Brothers, and even more surprised that some, like the elderly and charming Ceclia, regularly prayed for whomever was on Retreat!

The church, sometimes called the Chapel, was white walled with blonde wood supports and long opaque windows. A simple white marble altar had a panel in back of it that concealed the opening where the monks would come in. On either side of the altar were a set of pews for them to sit facing each other. Observing the season, the Chapel inside and outside was decorated with greenery and trees from their farm. It was so serene. Simple, fragrant and with the sense of "enough," while still lavish with the number of swags, ropes, and isolated trees. The trees became glorious wherever the sun touched them during the day as it moved from window to window in its path.

The whole community of Brothers would take part, and so there was a courteous waiting for the oldest ones to sidle into place. We saw our retreat leaders in a way that made any past flirtation seem a terrible recollection, never to be repeated! Time drew into itself and then there was nothing you could call *time*, just the sense of floating on the rich Plainsong that was tracing the air with melody. During Epiphany, I could hear the words I was accustomed to seeing in my Book of Common Prayer at home. Our gathered souls soared like a flock of birds unconcerned with destination, enjoying the gift of flight.

> All of us, then, should reflect seriously on how to appear
> before the majesty of God in the presence of his angels.
> That will make sure that, when we sing in choir, there
> is complete harmony between the thoughts in our mind
> and the meaning of the words we sing. _ RB 19

Those men always nailed RB 19 any time I was present! Being there for retreat during Epiphany was great, since it was a celebration of a shining light, of finding the Gift. The fact that it was a feast day meant the same songs and liturgy would be said, year after year, so I was never homesick for my own church. I could carry the soft sung melodies with me for most of the spring, tapping their depths of peace.

Incense was used in abundance here, fire alarms be banished! The Brother assigned as thurifer came forth and swung a brass censer on a long chain. He would thus bless the Bible, the altar, his Brothers, and us in the pews with grand arcs of the smoking golden globe. This was the monastic life: serving to the Glory of God, be it in the washing of dinner plates or the careful tending of the live coal, spooning the powdered incense over it at just the right time to produce fat billows of sweet smoke.

The God Box

...visit the sick and bury the dead.

_ *RB 4.2*

Alert readers may recall a brief mention of the "God Box" earlier. It was sort of like the Valentine's Day box from elementary school in ages past. There actually was a time when a child could choose or reject another without getting suspended for a day then sent for analysis. Into the wide slot of the God Box one could deposit offerings to our Higher Power. Over the course of the weekend it became filled with letters written before or during retreat, or a description of something we wanted to leave behind, maybe just a word or name on a scrap of paper. These were all part of the "letting go" work of retreating. We kissed our dropped opportunities up to God via the Box to rid them of the germs of memory.

Again, remembering the particular group I describe in this book, it was not unusual for other objects to be cast into the God Box. Retreat sisters would happily relate personal victories to table-mates over lunch: their dropping in a half-full pack of cigarettes, the name of a boss, or a picture of a past love (stabbed repeatedly with a screwdriver). It is another part of God's amazing grace how the deep pain of hours ago is soon replaced by giddy actions full of optimism and risk. On the last day of retreat we trooped outside to set the God Box on fire and let the smoke rise to Heaven, our version of the incense, I guess.

In the past, there had been times when the Box was stubborn and slow to catch afire. Perhaps that size 16 item in there...but we resourcefully solved this problem. *Sober women are creative.* More flammability was layered on by wrapping the Box in paper. From summer camping trips we discovered fire-starting aids and put them to a new use. Somebody finally remembered to pack charcoal lighter fluid. With these improvements you could have given God a *brick* and it would have eventually gone up in flames.

When all were gathered, a long match was poked into the Box. A little whoof! and it was soon engulfed by greedy fire. We formed a circle to sing Amazing Grace. We used the system of "lining" to get the lyrics out so we could hold hands as we sang. Lining is an old practice, allowing groups of people to sing without having to read or know the words. In lining, the person who does know the lyrics calls them out quickly in the small space between each line. It requires attention and a bit of memory from the group, and so the whole thing becomes a labor of devotion. After we sang, we silently watched the end of the burning, reflecting on what we had so brazenly done. We had embraced A.A.'s Step 3: made a decision to turn our wills and lives over to God as we understood Him.

Conspiracies of Love

To refrain from unnecessary speech and to guard our silence by not speaking until we are addressed. / The tenth step of humility teaches us not to be given to empty laughter on every least occasion…

_RB 7.16 & .17

Well, I'm afraid these two "instruments of good works" will surely keep most W-32 gals from the monastic life. We (noisy, loud) women are 180-degree people. If we aren't deep in silent meditation (which during Retreat can actually happen without the need to hide in the bathroom), we are *talkin'* y'all!

Yes! We <u>are</u> noisy and loud! We stomp, cheer and applaud; we practice quickly on Sunday morning so we can do "the wave" perfectly to honor our retreat leader as they end the conference. Occasional winter storms allowed us to display our sledding form, using trash can lids or heavy plastic bags. We leave no doubt about there being FUN in sobriety.

But of course we could rarely leave it at that. We began to develop a whole range of discussion group (remember the numbered, smaller groups?) activities to amuse ourselves, culminating with a Saturday night pooling of efforts. Lord help us, we did start out simply. First it was the Affirmations Bag. Sort of the opposite of the God Box, these brown paper lunch bags were meant to hold written declarations of some particular aspect we admired in another. The idea was you could read them later at home, and fondly recall your retreat sisters until we met again. There you go. Aside from the annual hiding of one particular member's bag just before she would go to pick it up, it was pretty calm and thoughtful.

The Affirmation Bags had our first name and initial, simply written with pencil or pen, and were clustered here and there in the big conference room. Then some women added their small group number - could have been more than one Sally G, so that was fine. But over the years we tacked on our home town, or our A.A. home-group's name. Hmmm… this could result in one's name getting lost in all that information. Can't have that! So the colored markers soon followed and then came gel pens, glitter, glue, poster paint and stickers. Now, this was just for our *names*. Somehow, or perhaps because of this urge to personalize, the gremlin of excess slipped into our small group assignments. They became more complex. Simple crafts made by each group – in itself a change viewed with suspicion by some - gradually evolved into tiny Broadway productions. This was *in addition* to the Affirmation Bags.

The year that in which a skit (yes, it got to that level) actually had my group forming a human basket, the year that many of us found ourselves packing enough craft items for a pre-school, the year that the hidden bag wound up on a ceiling fan blade, it all collapsed of its own weight. Thankfully, God allowed us to have fun while at the same time led us to form a collective resolve that the pendulum had swung as far as we should allow. Get back to just…retreating. But we do still have some pretty snazzy Affirmation Bags!

Our Dear Fr. Charles – An American Abbot

*It is above all important that monastic superiors should
not underrate or think lightly of the salvation of the souls
committed them by giving too much attention to transient
affairs of this world which have no lasting value.*

_RB 2:7

There was a gigantic but silent bell on a frame outside the rear entrance between the parking lot and the back of the dining hall. I wondered if it had been used back in the day, since monks out tending the fields of Christmas trees could have heard its toll easily. As I mentioned before, there were set hours for various times of praise, prayer and the like. "Prime" would have been noon time, and every few hours marked a point where the normal work would stop for the Brothers to assemble.

On some retreats I was willing to brave the cold, put my hard shoes back on and trudge all the way across the road and over to the church/ chapel. I would follow the walk off to the side that led to a smaller alcove where the monks gathered for their times of singing and chants, apart from Sunday service. I admit it was not often done, but even short exposure to this ancient practice offered a durable memory of serenity and holy purpose. It was a reminder that work was necessary and could even be a holy act, but it was always secondary to the praise and worship of God.

It was during the first time I sat and listened to the 6 pm evensong that I met Fr. Charles Coriston. I never thought to ask him if he served there as the Abbot. But by the presence he made I suspected he was, and later confirmed my guess. He was the first American to serve as Abbott, appointed in 1947, before I was born. I began retreats at the Abbey in 1989, and enjoyed many years of his hospitality to us guests. It was usually on Saturday afternoon that Fr. Charles slowly made his way over to the House from his office across the road. He mingled with us, hugged everybody, asked about relatives or former plans some had shared the year before. On later retreats, we observed somebody from the main building driving him over if the weather was especially bad. If not, they would walk with him to lend support if needed, especially for the risky Rt. 206 crossing. He rarely needed the support but was always grateful to the one who drew alongside and made it clear that there was no shame in asking for help. Fr. Charles was old, but with a sharp mind and great sense of humor. We all loved him.

I have a postcard of an aerial view of Queen of Peace that he sent me one year at Easter, and a little booklet of his called *"Proverbs and Sayings I Like,"* which has one of his own poems on aging. It was essentially a long prayer to be kept from the pull toward negativity, closed-mindedness, bitterness or self-pity at the increasing assaults of old age on body, mind and spirit. "A sour old person," he wrote, "is one of the crowning works of the devil." He didn't want that for himself or for others, so he wrote it and sent it out into the world. It is still a living, loving work of a man who knew the grace of God was for him to both receive and to share as encouragement, not condemnation.

One year I went up before retreat to volunteer as a helper during the Christmas tree sale, landing a nice spot in the small trailer where people paid for the tree. Volunteers were pretty well rewarded by hot cocoa at hand, and the invitation to take lunch in the dining area used by the usual occupants. Work went quickly since business was brisk, then we broke for lunch. As I hunched over my soup and bread in the dining hall feeling a little out of place, I was grateful when Charles appeared. He stopped by and we talked for a while. I was always impressed by his ability to remember us and even recall the time of year we typically came, since he joked "You're up early this year!" We stayed connected, and a couple of times I went to his office as an off-season visitor, enjoying his wisdom, his counsel and good advice. I learned he had authored some short essays I had seen elsewhere and admired. He gave me one of those colorful woven yarn strips used as a bracelet of friendship in South America. I brought him some possibly forbidden cookies I had baked. St. Benedict would have frowned on that, according to RB 54, *The Reception of Letters and Gifts in the Monastery*. But given the authority of the "superior," I figured if Fr. Charles *was* the Abbot there, then all was well! Heck, for all I know, he gave them as a present to somebody else, maybe his secretary or one of the cooks. When we give a gift, we should always free the giver to pass it on if they so desire. It's not a rejection of us at all, just passing our love on, giving it even more honor.

Abbott Fr. Charles died in the year 2000, just before we were scheduled to come up for retreat. I still had some books of his and was looking forward to returning them, but now there was no chance to say hello or goodbye. Another twist of life presented itself, another challenge to my ability to accept life on life's terms. This lesson involving the dear Charles established a new rule – Love Now – and I spent quite a bit of time at the Rock of Crosses that year. We stay connected by memory; we will meet again at the end of the age. May he rest in peace until that time, and rise in joyful triumph to receive his crown of glory.

CHAPTER 6

The Meeting With the Standing Committee of the Diocese of NJ

S t. George's Church was still following the pillars of cloud or fire marking God's path. Many exchanges of information, offers and prayer had occurred and more were anticipated. I had been Warden of the Vestry, gone back to being a Vestry member when that term ended, and spent my mandatory year off that we observed so nobody got too entrenched. By 2008, I was back in the Warden spot. In the former year as Jr. Warden, I was involved in the decision to select the group for our future affiliation. In that year, our Warden Mary and I were deep in setting timelines for committee actions, forming small groups to focus on particular tasks, and occasionally talking and praying with each other for wisdom. We were all on very new and unfamiliar turf and it was rough on the nerves, our family lives, pretty much everything.

There were a few groups we were considering: the Reformed Episcopal Church, CANA (Convocation of Anglicans in North America), and two others. We felt it important to act in the best interest of the whole parish since a priest could leave but the parish would remain. This required a lot of faith and humility on Fr. Bill's part but he was well equipped for the challenge. At St. George's it is the practice for Vestry votes to be unanimous, not just a majority. The thinking was that if the Holy Spirit was not speaking the same thing to all, then more was waiting to be said and the matter was tabled. But by this point we had little time for anything but prayer, decision, action, then back to prayer as each new matter popped up.

It was in 2008 that our meetings turned to true negotiation, and we prepared formal reports to fully unpack our side of the argument. We had the advice of a lawyer, of course, but what we wanted to do was appeal to a sense of fairness, justice and logic. Based on our experience, the Diocese was able to draft a formal protocol for what they called "disaffiliation." Point number 4 was the roadblock. Before we could proceed, it required the church to hand over the deed to its property. Could we trust this? Was it a trap?

As it was, we managed to work around No. 4. I'm still not sure how that happened, since "4" was sort of in the middle of the document, but we all kept talking and the legal fellows kept working. St. George's met the other requirements while defensively working on an escape plan, still with the legalistic requirement of no written communication to the parish. This was our chief regret and an obstacle to our normal way of operating. Parish members could ask us on the Vestry about the matter, but our preference had always been full communication, like that of a family.

This was probably one of the most difficult and painful aspects, not being able to work it out as a church family. Just the way it was, said the lawyer. But it was such a wrenching decision! In our church, it had meant something to be an Episcopalian. Our succession of priests knew the Bible and how to apply it to their own lives, and so they lived as examples. We cherished the beauty and seasonal framework of the Liturgy, and encouraged an awe of the Sacraments. And we cared about each other, kept the Great Commandments in mind and at hand as best we could. What was going to become of that part of our lives?

All of our past years of history with our Diocese competed in memory with the present years of conflict. We had always been supportive of the Bishops and the Diocese, even while being snickered at for our observance of tradition. Sorry, call us weird but we believed in the obligation to tithe, in the mandate to test our decisions against Scripture, to apply reason and not emotion to our choices. Now, we were "conservatives" and the snickering had turned to more articulate scoffing, or scattered moans of frustration at the annual Convention of the Diocese of NJ if our priest came up to the microphone for comment with Bible in hand.

Each step forward seemed like walking out in space. The pillar of fire was no more than a tiny spark now, but we could still see. We followed the pillar of cloud into the Bishop's office, then later into the meeting room where the whole Standing Committee waited to meet with Fr. Bill and his two Wardens. Mary had rotated off, so now it was Steve and I filling those spots. (He would be Warden by the time we would have our answer.)

The Big Day finally came and we presented our case. Outright ownership of all our property, granted in the Christian sense of "rightness" was our first request. This was an interesting position for me, since I had not been at the Vestry meeting where the decision to do that was taken. I really don't think I would have agreed with the it but sometimes God just moves us out of his way. Only one Vestry member was offering this choice yet all wound up adopting it for presentation at this meeting!

Amazingly, we were not cast out into the gutter after making this rather bodacious offer of…nothing, but predictably, this was rejected. We were going to have to have the property appraised. More money to spend, but we knew it was a meeting that could have had a much different outcome. The three of us left with an odd sense of calm following us to our cars. Departing the city of Trenton once again, onto Route 1 South back to Helmetta. We were still on the path, and still in our church. OK.

Not long afterward, Bishop Councell went off to climb a mountain – a big one. This was a symbol of his personal fight against Parkinson's and we kept him in prayer during his new challenge. God had either bought us some time, or was just fulfilling one of His reasons for creating the mountain. We would have to wait for the Bishop's return in January of 2009 before our offer could even be considered…so we waited.

CHAPTER 7

Leaving the Abbey

RB 68:1- The Response to Orders That Seem Impossible

If instructions are given to anyone in the community which seem too burdensome, or even impossible, then the right thing to do is accept the order in a spirit of uncomplaining obedience. However...

It was during the business meeting of Matt Talbot Group W-32's retreat that we learned we would have to leave Newton – January of 2001. Everything started to whirl around in my mind. Grieving the land, the pond yet unreached, and how, without the Rock of Crosses, could it all really ever work, this business of Retreating?

...if the burden of this task appears to be completely beyond the strength of the monk or nun to whom it has been assigned, then there should be no question of a rebellious or proud rejection, but it would be quite right to choose a good opportunity and point out gently to the superior the reasons for thinking that the task is really impossible.

We continued our meeting with as much order as we could in our state of shock, in the way people make arrangements for a funeral after a sudden death. Of course, gatherings of groups in the Matt Talbot Retreat Movement were conducted in many fine retreat houses. Several of our members knew of other locations and offered them for our consideration, voices trailing off toward the end with a barely-audible sigh. Normally we would have launched heartily into debating the pros and cons of each, but this was a conversation that none of us wanted to have.

My last visit to the Rock of Crosses was spent staring silently at the testimonies of decades of people sitting in this same spot. My own crosses were there, too. They could not be uprooted since they had already been crafted, offered over the years and left behind along with their crucified intentions of the day. Messages of hope for the unseen others; it was not *my* Rock, after all. But it meant so much to me! Could it all really ever work again?

September 11, 2001 came along several months later. Without any doubt, 2001 was definitely *not* the best year for those of us who were livin' in the USA.

If the superior, after listening to this submission, still insists on the original command, then the junior must accept that it is the right thing and, with loving confidence in the help of God, obey.

Xavier Center - Holy Hide and Seek
(You Are Cold as Ice!)

We should remember, however, that such obedience will be acceptable
to God and rewarding to us if we carry out the orders given us in
a way that is not fearful, nor slow, nor halfhearted, nor marred by
murmuring or the sort of compliance that betrays resentment.

_RB 5.4

Da Bronx and Long White Gloves: Women of Steel

It is January of 2002, on the campus of the College of St. Elizabeth at Convent Station, New Jersey. Our retreat's trusted servants have found and booked us into the Xavier Center, and so here we sit on Friday evening, waiting.

Sister Eileen enters the large, subfloor room. The whole of W-32 is in a big semicircle, neither noisy nor loud, holding a collective breath. Eileen is stocky with short hair and briefly reminds me of Winston Churchill without the cigar (maybe it's upstairs). After taking a long moment to look us over, she informed us that there are only two places in the entire world that start with "the" – Bronx and Vatican – and she has lived in or visited both. This gets some scattered short laughs, cracking if not breaking the ice and we start to breathe out.

Then, in comes Nancy. We hold our collective breath again. She comes in carefully bearing a tray of bulbs, the kind you *plant*, and a soft murmur of suspicion snakes through the seated women. Frankly, most of W-32 is a crowd that would average a little low on the "dainty" scale.

Nancy is tall compared to Eileen and carries a whiff of Good Housekeeping formality along with her offering, an aura of long gowns and white gloves. We move barely more than our eyes as we trace the tray's progress to the front of the room. She sets it down and the tiny *clack*! of its contact with the Formica table top explodes like a gunshot in our thick and sullen silence.

Plus, there is something else. It's <u>cold</u> – the big room we're in is partly underground with a terrazzo floor, glossy beige cinderblock walls and could have swallowed our Abbey's conference room. This incoming tray of *flower* bulbs is a bad sign to some of us who are feeling like livestock being herded up a ramp for the last time. Nancy's voice is soft, to some condescending, and a common sense of our facing a very loooong weekend starts to harden our hearts. Some fold their arms. I do the same...hey, it's *cold* in here!

Holy Hide and Seek - The Stations Path (You're Getting Warmer!)

As soon as decently possible, I have to get out of there. Need to walk. Moving unnoticed through a group of quietly complaining smokers out on the designated deck, I first survey the manicured grounds from this vantage point.

Downhill there is a big graveyard by the parking area, some patches of woods, and the many buildings that surround Xavier Center.

Wanting to burn off some negative energy, I head up the steep hill. It's not something my body appreciates but has to be done, says the doctor. Exercise as opposed to work seems pointless to me but in this setting it was the perfect outlet. I feel like I'm being watched; we are after all on the grounds of a richy-rich girls' college. All the buildings, no matter what vintage, are huge and imposing. Grassy expanses stretch out, ringed by thin woods. I imagine in one of the buildings a phalanx of Security personnel seated before a bank of monitors. Their eyes narrow at the sight of me, a non-student, non-Sister blue-collar life form wandering their tidy campus.

Up, up the hill I labor on, back the way we drove in, down a hill and then up another. Rounding a curve I spot an old wooden sign to the right, and take the direction of its fading black arrow.

Coming into an area clearly meant for the maintenance supplies and vehicles, I think I've gone wrong then see the start of a (designated) walk, heading into the woods. Everything here is "assigned"! Smoke here, walk there…but maybe I just need to crank up the acceptance factor, eh?

I march on, and it turns out to be a Stations of the Cross path, complete with large statues and cement sitting benches. The snow lies unmarked by human Walkers…until this one. Pillar of cloud! I take the comforting path my Abbot has shown me, and soak in a long meditative walk broken by times of sitting and letting the hard things come to mind then go away, released. I return to the retreat center with a **bit** more gratitude in the attitude. But we still have a whole day and a half in this place! Time never mattered at the Abbey…ugh!

Holy Hide and Seek - The Labyrinth
(You're Getting Hot!)

While in San Francisco on a business trip, exploring during some down time, I visited St. Paul's Cathedral. Inside, a section of the expansive space accommodated a Labyrinth – a circular set of narrow paths that serve as a meditative walk. Of course, there are *rules* so I check them out...take shoes off...you can stop and even sit on the floor if you like but leave room for others to pass...keep silence. OK, got it. A beautiful time, very peaceful, then back to the hotel.

Here, back inside Xavier after the Stations Path walk, it is still free time and I wander around the House in my restless way. It's a new place and I need to overcome the newness. I find the same circular configuration laid out as a huge carpet in a big room at the very end of a hall. Nobody else is around. I start walking *this* Labyrinth, and God shows up.

Like Life, the walk seems pretty easy at the start when we're kids. You decide what you want to be when you grow up, and head that way, toward Center. Then *real* Life begins to happen. Some of us carry the seeds of a physical, mental and spiritual malaise, one of the "isms" like alcoholism, for example. These explode, reach the surface and sprout. Our straight path zings away to the side, we lose sight of Center, we circle around the edge of what others seem to easily obtain. We walk on, but get so very far away – away from family then friends then job then away from the "us" we once loved and cherished. We are lost but keep shuffling along, head down, feet scraping the sidewalk as we head for the bar, or to our kitchen table for another drink from the hidden bottle before the kids or the husband get home.

A Labyrinth offers us the chance to do that whole lousy journey again, in one compact space, and to feel the pain of every single, rotten choice we ever made. Great!

At some point on the narrow path I suddenly recall the day of my first marriage's divorce, and weep, but keep walking. Around another tight curve on the path I recall my first A.A. meeting, while I was still in the detox in South Amboy. Teasingly close to Center again, the path zags in the opposite direction. In obeying the order for this second walk, I come to understand. Now I feel again the purposeful turning away from recovery that I chose time and again, running from Salvation back to the slavery of bottle or line. *My* choices, mine alone.

We will not regret the past, nor wish to shut the door on it (Alcoholics Anonymous, p. 83). I see the promise of A.A. founders Bill and Bob right under my feet as I draw near to completing the Labyrinth walk. Finally I have come to the end and am permitted to step into the round, flower-like Center. I stand there, a woman of a certain age, looking out one of the windows at a slice of the winter landscape. I am just a dot on Earth. I suddenly realize how wonderful it is, to be alive. I feel blessed with Purpose. Hmmm…maybe I can even "do" this weekend…eh, God?

Holy Hide & Seek – A Rocky Way
(You're on Fire!)

It's the late afternoon of Saturday, our first full day here. Exhausted by hours of conflicting feelings and reactions, I go off on another walk but in the opposite direction. Heading down the hill toward the parking lot, I'm expecting nothing in particular since this area leads down toward a main road then out. The large cemetery to my left seems off limits and I pause, mid-hill, to scan the potential for walking. There is some kind of monument or *something* that attracts my attention, off by itself as an island in the frosted green lawn. I head down that way. Getting a little closer with each step, I see that it's…a big pile…of… rocks.

I saunter down, still on sidewalk, and then come around the side of it. On my approach, I was facing the back of the structure, and now feel a familiar sensation, the hand of an angel at my back ushering me gently around. I pass under an arch and am now inside the structure of an elaborate, stony memorial. Then I see it; there is a cross in the rocks!

Humility is nothing like *humiliation*. Humility is what I feel while beholding this sight. Sanitized as it is in this academic setting, I know for sure by this third sign that my Abbott has chosen this retreat place. I stand before a transformed Rock of Crosses, brought here to soften my heart to the Xavier Center. Even I can't miss this gesture and all it implies. Pillar of fire, pillar of cloud as God provided, then led me to his perfect substitute for each part of the Abbey that I had treasured and thought lost in my limited understanding. They were not the same as the former ones, just as my next day on earth will not be the same as today. They were simply different. Instead, I was given the gift of acceptance, the Abbot's release to continue our journey in <u>this</u> place, which is the amazement we find in God's grace.

Now this cold, dead place is coming alive! Here and there I can see little additions tucked into the rocks. Maybe they will blow away, maybe the army of groundskeepers will come and clear them off from time to time, but for now they serve my Lord's good purpose. I feel His very smile as I place a small stone picked from the Stations Path inside the larger jumble, and turn away. I start back uphill, to a new Jerusalem. I will humbly serve in any way He provides for me here, in my new retreat house, my Abbey.

RB 7:20 – A new motive will have taken over, not fear of hell but the love of Christ. Good habit and delight in virtue will carry them along. This happy state the Lord will bring about through the Holy Spirit in his servant, whom he has cleansed of vice and sin and taught to be a true and faithful worker in the kingdom.

No Longer Seeking But Finding

By this time in my recollections, my memory is pushing many of the Xavier Center retreats together. My scant record, kept penciled in a small booklet I got with my Medallion, shows 2002 as our first year there. But I do remember this: we are dancing.

Maybe it was that first year with Nancy, maybe it was her at a different time, or it could have been later with another leader, maybe Robin? Who cares – maybe you remember and can start your own book!

"*We are home now*" was the collective mood in the big, cold room. We all felt the Abbot's permission and released our pent-up sorrows. Young and old, dancer and plodder, we are holding hands in a circle and moving as one, smiling at each other with a new joy. Even later in the night, the larger group broken up and some already asleep, music and dancing continue. We are noisy, loud sober women self-controlled by letting ourselves go along with the Spirit's new song, intoxicated with the freedom only found in movement. Nobody *cares* about looking good, nobody *cares* if our partner absolutely cannot dance, for everybody has come to accept that we, Group W-32, are home. And we are dancing!

CHAPTER 8

Finding My Place: The Altar of Wholeness & Broken-ness

The third step of humility is to submit oneself out of love of God to whatever obedience under a superior may require of us; it is the example of the Lord himself that we follow in this way…

_RB 7.9

"**C**an you fill in for the evening meditation?"

This was the question placed before me by one of our trusted servants, the core of W-32's leadership. Apparently some respite was needed for our retreat leader who was with us for the first time and experiencing the full force of alcoholic unburdening. The request was fine with me; service to others is what recovery should be about. Plus, as the "liner" of *Amazing Grace* when we fired up the God Box, I had obtained a tiny niche for myself and apparently my Abbot had a new job to add. OK. I headed upstairs to my room to prepare, considering myself a cracked clay pot that could yet be of use. In a state of broken-ness, which I like to write that way to remind myself of the potential to reach wholeness, I can allow something of my Higher Power to enter my vessel. What would it be? I feel a bit of excitement as I close the door of my room.

The rooms here were a little different than those in the Abbey in that there was usually no sink present, but the general sparseness was familiar. During the day the sleeping rooms were colder than I would have liked, but towels make a fine lap robe. I had been part of a mission-minded church long enough to know that Americans live in incredible, thoughtless luxury. That started a train of thought that I followed while randomly reading Psalms and Proverbs. After a while I felt the preparation was over. Topic & focus: gratitude.

At Xavier Center, if you come in the front door rather than the designated smoking area (by this time I had also accepted the higher degree of structure here), to the right were two heavy doors with stained glass panels that opened to the Chapel. It was much larger than the little upstairs Abbey chapel, more like a church and quite grand in comparison. In between the pew area and the Communion rail was a table-like stone altar. Modern worship brings the Celebrant much closer to the People. I decided to take a risk and use this as a point of delivery – it gave me more confidence and I hoped it would lend some authority to my reflections. Alcoholics need to be especially careful of situations like these – one false move and you think it's all about you! Or somebody else *thinks* you think so.

As it turned out, I was able to get out of my own way, praise God! Nobody seemed to feel cheated by another W-32 member leading the meditation. That was the first and last time I felt the need to shelter behind the little altar. Over the past few years I've had the chance to repeat the experience, and God got the message through no matter where I stood. Take a risk, step up to a challenge – no effort for God is wasted!

Finding the Bathtubs – Holy Water

*The monastery itself should be constructed so as to include
within its bounds all the facilities which will be needed, that is,
water, a mill, a garden and workshops for various crafts.*

_RB 66.2

Retreat houses generally offered shared bathrooms situated in the middle and near the end of each sleeping area. At Xavier, some of these were devoted to showers only, a frustrating discovery if you had something else in mind. It was a year or two before I realized that some also featured womanly wonders of the world: deep bathtubs. A bathtub offers the highest form of relaxation, thus the one most often denied by women in order to keep pace with our crazy lives. But this was retreat — Fill 'er up!

While the tub filled I flew downstairs to the break area and prepared a cup of tea. Treading the fine line between wasting water (a precious gift as several posted prayers in the tub room reminded me) and wanting to have a nice therapeutic soak, I kept the level moderate but cranked up the heat. Returning with my tea, a bundle of dry clothes, soap and facial scrub, I oo-ouched my way lower and lower into the steamy water. Aahhhhh.

John the Baptist was busy dunking those lined up in the river for a "cleansing" that was a ritual of his day, sort of like Saturday afternoon Confession. He is yelling at the sinners on the shore still holding back and talking trash to the religious right who had plenty of scroll-knowledge but little conception of mercy. Suddenly he looks up to see his cousin Jesus heading his way. He probably felt the way I did when asked, "Can you fill in?" In fact, the Bible relates that's exactly how he <u>did</u> feel – but Jesus reassures him that it's cool. The prophets of old knew He was going to be stepping into that water and He meant to honor the visions they had been given by the Father. Jesus came up out of the water, was blessed by the Holy Spirit and all hell did indeed break out, but in defeat (Matt. 3)

That's what the water of baptism is for – and although I was a long way from my infant days, the power of water was not lost on me now. The soothing warmth, the soaping and the rinsing, the luxury of time to just get clean! In offering for this wonder, one could think of the homeless and pray, or of the people who must walk miles to get just one jug of water, and pray. And so the water used in this manner was never truly wasted. I'm an American – I was put here and so I shouldn't feel guilty about my resources, but I do have an obligation to share my blessings. Prayer begins the process since it's an act of the will. With heart opened, the ready instruction and inspiration from God meant just for this one begin to flow in and create generosity. An image or an idea may form. If acted upon or remembered later in the day and carried out, the result is an active faith, one the produces work for the Kingdom of God.

I rise from the tub and start the drain gurgling, dedicating the hour past to my good God and asking Him to pour out this blessing on my "twin." Someplace in the world I believe we all have one, somebody who lives an opposite life from mine in deep poverty and need, but who is also hoping, praying and praising the same God. I pray she finds at hand everything she needs for her family this day, as I dress and return to my retreat sisters who are gathered and talking, blessing each other with fellowship. I pray she also comes upon some special wonder, something she had hardly dared hope to attain. I send her Love Now, and receive a sure sudden surge of joy and something like relief.

CHAPTER 9

We Are Still Here

It is summertime of 2007 and I am working as Sexton at St. George's part time, cleaning the church and its meeting hall. Things are in limbo at my full time job with a new and unwelcome union starting to form. Our normal salary increases are frozen in the meantime and a little more money was needed. This is the perfect side job, since I live close enough to walk over. Nobody else is around as I punch in and head upstairs. The church is still and its stained glass windows blaze from the July sun. I polish the dark wood and pick bits of old wax off pew cushions, left behind from winter service celebrations of the Light of the World. Every year we risked all as a scattering of young children in the congregation held lighted candles along with the adults while a very looong hymn concluded the service in our lovely old church.

I think of the old Abbey as I work and of the wooden ceiling of the dining hall with its shining deep brown panels and beams. I wonder what the inside of the House is like now, wonder if the dust has been allowed to settle and coat the surfaces of sills and chairs, tables and desks. I hope not, but think maybe so. Or perhaps all the furnishings are gone. God has taken away the pain of such recollections, leaving only a soft regret that my humanity still chooses to embrace. Progress, not perfection, as we say in A.A.

The Vestry is caught up in a flurry of activity, forming new teams around the many and increasing details of our proposed separation from ECUSA. Will we need to find a temporary worship place? We hope not, since all of the places we had found available so far seem rather puny. All of our written records, many bound as very old ledgers showing names and dates of baptism…what about those? The lawyer was advising us along the way and occasionally bringing up possibilities that disturb our composure. But we forge ahead anyway. We make copies, move records to CDs, and keep sorting it all out.

Our ability to communicate to the parish, at least in writing, is still hamstrung. "Nothing in writing!" cries the lawyer. No email, no newsletter updates…but we are still here and doing our best as we wait.

Pillar of Fire: The Standing Committee and the Settlement Offer

Renounce your own desires and ambitions so as to be free to follow Christ.

_RB 4.2

The Bishop of the Diocese of New Jersey had come down from the mountain.

It is late in 2008. We on the Vestry had agonized over "the number," the actual amount we would offer to purchase what the deed in our safe described. The appraisal of our property had come in at 1.7 million bucks. Fortunately, only a couple of weeks later the economic meltdown lopped off about a third of that value, showing that in every bad there's a bit of good for somebody. Our deed to the property was essentially a piece of historic paper. Church law and Canon stated that a church's property was held in trust for the Diocese, and that was that. This matter of Canon law had gone as high up in the courts as it ever would, and that was the hard fact that came down. If the Standing Committee didn't accept our offer we would have to find another place; we'd be paying them, or paying a landlord.

A few years past, the Bishop had hinted at some possible financial agreement, and so we decided to go at least twice over that figure, stringing out the payments over time. A lot of time. If they raised "the number," perhaps we could just extend the term. On the horizon of our thought was the specter of the Presiding Bishop – would she swoop in like a vulture and put complications on the whole deal? Would it fall through? Would the Standing Committee not see us making a "first" and therefore flexible offer or miss that intention and reject it outright?

So many questions…would humanity *ever* learn to trust God?

For more than 15 years now I've had one of those perpetual calendars on my desk at work. Instead of one set year, there are daily pages on a spiral binding to flip over. This particular one has the theme of "spiritual warfare." Some of the pages have Bible verses, but others are bits of song or hymn lyrics and such. I admit I've always preferred the Bible verse dates.

On January 14, 2009 I was scheduled to meet Steve, the incoming Warden, at his house after work to place my signature along with his and that of Fr. Bill on our formal offer to the Standing Committee. The calendar reading for this date was from 2 Chronicles 20:17: "You will not need to fight in this battle; take your position, stand still, and see the victory of the Lord on your behalf, O Judah and Jerusalem. Fear not, and be not dismayed…"

When a day brings some extraordinary circumstance I tend to make a note on the page. My calendar now bears a reminder of what I signed; maybe a later date will have a note about the outcome. But it's out of our hands now. Originally we thought we would be at the meeting when they considered the offer, but learned that would not be the case. So we scheduled a time of prayer in the church during the two hours when the Standing Committee would meet in Trenton. By this time even the town's founding Helme family was joined with us in prayer, so Helmetta's petitions to God for justice were joined with others in New York, Florida, and Rhode Island. We would obey, take up our positions and stand firm. By now, everybody in the parish was willing to walk away if it came to that. Acceptance of things we could not change by ourselves had settled in our hearts. We were finally free in Spirit, and had our peace. We waited on the Lord.

Xavier Center, Retreating Again - Big Bag, Comin' Through!

The fifth step of humility is that we should not cover up but humbly confess to our superior or spiritual guide whatever evil thoughts come into our minds and the evil deeds we have done in secret. This is what scripture urges on us when it says: Make known to the Lord the way you have taken and trust in him. Psalm 36:5

_RB 7.12

Today is January 15th, 2009. Tomorrow, God willing, I will be loading up my car with my sponsee Nancy's trademark big bag. We will find room for Kim's luggage next to my own, and head north up Rt. 287 to Xavier Center. Not so far up as Newton, but close enough. It was time for Retreat!

W-32 almost got shut out this year, a consequence of the same economic meltdown that shrunk St. George's property assessment. Only a scant few sent in their reservations when the form went out in October. Usually we dash to the mailbox while writing out the check to ensure a place. Actually, the registration dip was not surprising for a women's retreat, or so we heard from one of the men's groups. The demands of family, medical issues or the loss of jobs hit us women harder and often limits our ability to spend freely. We had also been informed that the Xavier Center could not accommodate more than about seventy of us this year so perhaps that was a factor as well. But it all pulled up like a cartoon jet moments before crashing and we were on!

During the business meeting we'll discuss the problem and maybe it will have us looking for another retreat house. RB 7:8 advises: "The second step of humility is not to love having our own way nor delight in our own desires." As the *Rule* draws to its close in chapter 73.2, Benedict states his view that the life his work described was but a beginning on the road to "…greater heights of monastic teaching and virtue in the works which we have mentioned above, and with God's help you will then be able to reach those heights yourself. Amen." And we in recovery know that this is possible, too. We have seen, heard and described exactly such miracles that came after making a decision and doing the work of recovery in partnership with the Higher Power of our understanding of the time. Each item in the God Box, each affirmation dropped into a retreat sister's bag, each hour spent listening or being heard, each stab of regret or glimmer of hope, each rough cross giving silent testimony of belief in any circumstance, all of these offerings of self were instantly made holy, placed into capable hands.

It is clear that Benedict of Nursia was a wise child of God who knew that he was also on a journey along with all those under his care. Benedict relied upon the virtues of trust, obedience and humility, and so did Matt Talbot of Ireland. And somehow, coffee and all, we lovely ladies will be permitted to gain more of those qualities from this year's Retreat, and hope to pass them along to another.

Extreme cold is predicted for the days ahead. But it will be hot enough in that big cold room once we (noisy, loud) Group W-32 women get together again. Together in spirit with those not present this time, grateful to be here with each other and most certainly joined by fire with the Abbot who loved Matt Talbot and all of us into sobriety, charity and freedom. Never give up on your journey to the "greater heights" Dear Reader, because great is His faithfulness!

EPILOGUE

2009

Xavier Center – Sister Eileen was once again an excellent retreat leader, and dance we did! We will return in 2010, God willing, and I was asked to be the Retreat Leader. Amazing Grace, how sweet the sound, when dreams come true like these!

St. George's Anglican Church - The Standing Committee did not reject our last offer. We move into a negotiation period. The Presiding Bishop will be the next hurdle, but we are at peace with God's will. We gratefully behold the pillars of fire and cloud that have never faded. On April 26, 2009, we held our first Recovery Sunday – celebrating lives changed and saved from addiction. So you see, the paths have crossed!

2010

Rev. Bill Guerard announces the final acceptance of our offer by the Standing Committee to a congregation seated and holding its collective breath. A shocked moment of silence, then cheers, tears, applause, praise shouted and dust falling from the ceiling fans! A mortgage will be drawn up, and we will move on in gratitude for the miracles of God. Our successful disaffiliation made a mark in history yet we remain in prayer that we won't be the only congregation to succeed. But, so far, it's just us. Watch and pray. All they want is to remain faithful to tradition, Scripture and reason, but churches continue to be sued by ECUSA and face eviction. Should it happen I know that each parish will find that Our Lord is waiting on the other side of the wall to start their new journey. Do not fear, but rejoice that your names are written on His heart. Amen?

REFERENCES

Websites

www.StGeorgesHelmetta.org

St. George's Anglican Church, 56 Main Street, Helmetta NJ 08828

www.matttalbotretreats.org

History and present-day information on Matt Talbot and spiritual retreats for recovering alcoholics

www.cana.org

The Convocation of Anglicans in North America

www.Virtueonline.org

Maintained by Mr. David Virtue, chronicles the current and past conflicts within the Episcopal Church of the USA, especially during the 2005-2010 period

Books

Barry, Patrick O.S.B. Saint Benedict's Rule. Mahwah: Hidden Spring, 2004

Kardong, Terrence G. O.S.B. Day by Day with St. Benedict. Collegeville: Liturgical Press, 2005

Alcoholics Anonymous. New York: Alcoholics Anonymous World Services, Inc., 3rd ed., 1976

Twelve Steps & Twelve Traditions. New York: Alcoholics Anonymous
   World Services, Inc., 1985

The Old and New Testaments of The Holy Bible, Revised Standard
   Version. Second ed. Dallas: Melton Book Co., 1971. Print.

CPSIA information can be obtained at www.ICGtesting.com
Printed in the USA
BVOW070253120413

317842BV00006B/2/P